Dating, Courtship and Betrothal

Sorting Our Marriage Matters with Bible Principles

by

Douglas Hammett

Dating, Courtship, and Betrothal

Sorting Our Marriage Matters With Bible Principles

by
Douglas Hammett

ISBN# 978-0-86645-283-0

All Scripture quotations taken from King James Version

Printed in the United States of America

Challenge Press
4702 Colebrook Avenue
Emmaus, PA 18049
610-965-4700
www.lvbaptist.org

Table of Contents

Chapter One
The Surest Way to Destroy Your Future Marriage

When you look at the title of this chapter, you might think it a little strange. I realize that anyone in their right mind does not desire to destroy their marriage—whether present or future. Hopefully you want to avoid that at all costs. But that is what many young people in our world today are doing.

Therefore this is a very key subject for many of your lives, especially the young people that are looking towards marriage someday. It is also important for parents who desire to raise their children and point them in a right direction. If you are past all those stages, you still ought to be concerned about younger people that you can influence—whether in your church or in your neighborhood or in your family.

George Barna recently published a troubling survey. He found that 27% of marriages where both the husband and wife claim to be a Christian end in divorce. In that same survey he showed that Roman Catholics have a lower percentage than those who claim to be Christians, and atheists have a much lower divorce rate at only 21%. As God's people, we should be upset at these figures.

I believe the reason for these disturbing statistics is because there is something that is wrong today—in the Christian community, in our churches, in our Bible colleges—and it is destroying families and marriages. I just want to warn you that this is a very unusual topic—but if you will examine it carefully, I think you will agree that it is Biblical and it is needed in our society today.

"Furthermore then we beseech you, brethren, and exhort you by the Lord Jesus, that as ye have received of us how ye ought to walk and to please God, so ye would abound more and more.

For ye know what commandments we gave you by the Lord Jesus.

For this is the will of God, even your sanctification, that ye should abstain from fornication.

That every one of you should know how to possess his vessel in sanctification and honour.

Not in the lust of concupiscence, even as the gentiles which know not God.

That no man go beyond and defraud his brother in any matter: because the Lord is the avenger of all such, as we also have forewarned you and testified.

For God hath not called us unto uncleanness, but unto holiness.

He therefore that despiseth, despiseth not man, but God, who hath also given unto us his holy Spirit." (First Thessalonians 4:1-8)

Let's look at these verses and see what Paul is teaching us here. Paul had only spent about four weeks in the city of Thessalonica, and yet in the time that he was there, he taught them how they should live—not only by mouth but by example.

Verses One through Three

In verse one he says they should be walking in a way that pleases God. That is how our Christian life should be. We should be more concerned about pleasing God than we are about pleasing anyone else.

Paul states in verses two and three that while he was with them there in Thessalonica, he taught them the commandments of Jesus Christ. One of those commandments was that they were to abstain from fornication, and they were to live a life of sanctification and honor. The word *sanctification* simply means *holiness*. God wants us as Christian to live a holy life—but it is not always easy.

If you look around our nation—on the television, on the billboards, on the radio, in the periodicals in the store—in all these you see moral impurity. It is everywhere in our society today. Sadly, in many independent Baptist churches, immorality reigns. Thankfully, we are not as bad as the world—but we like to look at how bad the world is and stay a few steps behind them. And we will be OK with one another—but not OK with God.

Verse Four

If you want to abstain from fornication, God gives you the answer. The word *vessel* is talking about the body in which you live. You need to know how to control your own body.

But First Peter chapter three says that the wife you marry is a vessel. The Bible also talks about two people becoming one flesh when they marry. So this verse is not just talking about how to possess my own vessel—how to operate within my own body—but it is also referring to the vessel that I acquire through marriage—my wife. This verse is teaching us about marriage.

God's Word teaches us that there is a holy way to go about getting a wife and getting to the marriage altar. And most of us did not get there in sanctification and honor. If we are honest about it, we would have to admit that the way we went about getting married was not a holy way.

No one ever taught me how to go about getting married in a holy way, so I just did what everyone else did. I used my own wisdom and my own ways, and sprinkled a little Bible in with it. And I think most people looking at my wife and I would say, "Oh, aren't they a wonderful Christian couple? They look so good." But we did not get to the marriage altar in a way that could be called a holy way.

In verse four, God says that we each need to possess our vessel in holiness and honor. Young men, to honor means that you value the young lady that you are going to marry. You appreciate her in a way that is befitting of her value. So you need to be asking yourself,

"How am I going to find a wife in a way that shows that I value her highly?"

Ladies, I want you to think back when you were younger, and remember how you used to think about getting married. Did you dream of some guy that looked like a cave man coming along and hitting you over the head with his club and then dragging you off to marry him?

No, more than likely you had some kind of vision of a knight in shining armor that would come rushing in and rescue you, and then take you away to marry you. You wanted someone to honor and cherish you.

Men, wouldn't it be something if we could get to the marriage altar in a way that befits holiness, and speaks loudly to the woman we marry that she is highly treasured? Wow, I tell you what—that would make a big difference in a marriage. I don't know any woman that would turn her nose up at that. Most women desire that and would do all they could to please that man that so highly treasures them.

Men, if you really want a wife that will go all out for you, here is what you do. Treat her with great distinction and honor. It won't happen overnight, because at first she will think that you are after something and she will be suspicious of your motives. But eventually she will see that you are genuine—and she will give her all to please you.

Verse Five

In verse five, Paul talks about the lust of concupiscence—which is a craving desire. Now I hate to use this term, but it is kind of like dogs that are in heat. You may think that is disgusting, but if you have watched young people today, there is a great similarity between the two.

The lust of concupiscence says, "I have got to have this girl. I have got to have this guy. This is what I want. I have got to have it." Parents see it happening and want to stop it but they don't know how. Young people are out of control.

Sadly, there is no difference between the Christians and the rest of the world in that matter. Christians are acting like they don't know God. I was shocked recently when I was introduced to a website with some pictures of an independent Baptist church's youth group. The pictures were of the young people in the church, including the pastor's children. There were many pictures of boys and girls physically hanging all over each other.

I thought how sad that the pictures looked so much like those of the world. Yet they claimed to be Christian young people. That is the way of the world, not the way of God. What a sad commentary! I would not expect anything different out of the world—but I do expect something different out of God's people. And I desire something better for your children.

During Paul's day, Greek culture had a double standard. Women were expected to marry their husband, be chaste and submissive to their husband, and to stay at home and raise the children. But it was different for the men. The husband was allowed to travel all over, alone.

It was socially acceptable for him to visit the brothels while he was away from home. The brothels set up throughout the country were next to the temples, and the profits from the brothels were used to worship their false deities. It was a wicked and twisted society.

Yet Paul made it very clear that there was to be a difference between the way the Christians acted and the way the lost Gentiles acted. He warned them to guard themselves against the influence of the wicked society all around them. In our society today, we need to do the same thing.

Let me ask you a question—how do those in the world go about getting a wife? How do they get to the marriage altar—and what parts of that should you avoid?

As a parent, what parts of that should you carefully guard your children from and keep them from practicing? Remember, God says you are to get to the marriage altar in sanctification and honor of that young lady that you may be marrying.

Verse Six

In verse six, the words *go beyond* speaks of certain boundaries that are marked off, and no man should step over those boundaries. Who draws the boundaries? It is not Mom and Dad, but it is God that draws the limits. He is the one that draws the boundaries.

In verse six also, Paul speaks about *defrauding*. To defraud means to go in to get your way with someone else. It also has the idea of promising something that you are not going to fulfill. The term *brother* is a generic term, meaning another Christian—a brother or sister in Christ. They are someone who is in Christ and they are to be treated as such.

Paul also gives us a warning in verse six—the Lord is the avenger of all such. That ought to scare you down to your boots. If you defraud a brother or sister in Christ, you have to answer to God for your actions. I think it is interesting to note that in the four weeks that Paul was with these people in Thessalonica, he had taught them and warned them about the consequences if they disregarded the boundaries that God had set in this matter of how to get to the marriage altar. This is a very important subject.

Verses Seven and Eight

In verse 7, the word *uncleanness* speaks of sexual impurity and wrong thinking. God has not called us as Christians unto uncleanness, but unto holiness.

Paul knew that there were going to be some that would not like what he was saying. But in verse 8 he warned them that their problem was not with him but with God. Moral purity is the will of God.

What exactly is defrauding and how is it affecting marriages today? I want to look at that subject in the next chapter.

Chapter Two
The Sin of Defrauding

I heard the story about the pastor of a large church in America. One night they were having a revival service at the church, and during the invitation a lady came and asked to talk to him after the service. When they sat down to talk, the lady told him that she loved him.

At first, he didn't understand what she was talking about, but finally realized that she was saying that she was in love with him, even though he was a married man. This lady was definitely involved in defrauding. We will look a little later at how the pastor handled that situation—and I think it will be a very instructive matter for us.

Definition of Defrauding

I want to look a little more at the definition of the word *defrauding* that we saw in First Thessalonians 4:6. The word defraud is found 5 times in our New Testament. Two times it is translated as *make a gain*, two times as *defraud*, and one time as *get an advantage*. It has the idea behind it of taking something away from someone, or depriving a person of something.

It means to cheat or deceive, or to overreach the boundary that is properly ours and take something away from someone and get an unfair advantage of them. In other words, to get a greater share than what we deserve. To put it together in a statement it would be like this: *to defraud is to take that which is not yours to take, while implying to promise something that you cannot give in exchange.*

Four Words

There are four words that describe defrauding in the context of the passage in First Thessalonians chapter four. We want to look at each of these words and what it means in the issue of defrauding.

Sly

First, to defraud has the idea of being sly. Paul speaks of going beyond. It means doing something that is deceitful—to do something for your own gain but not tell the other person that it is for your gain. You want them to think that it is for them.

Selfishness

Second, to defraud has the idea of selfishness. Verse 5 makes that very clear. The *lust of concupiscence* is that strong desire for something that is not rightfully yours. It is a desire and a craving that causes you to want it so much that it is motivated by selfishness. It becomes a violation of the second great commandment—to love your neighbor as yourself.

In Philippians chapter two Paul says that we should look on the things of others, and not on the things of ourselves. That is a hard way to live—in fact, it is impossible to live that way consistently unless you are a child of God.

We are selfish creatures ever since the fall in the Garden of Eden. When we want something, we can even deceive ourselves into believing it is for the best of the other person, when it is really for us—for our own cravings and lust.

The lust of concupiscence is seen when the young man says, "I want what I want out of you, and if I don't get what I want out of you, I am not going to have anything to do with you anymore. I am through with you." Young lady, if you ever hear those words from a young man, it is a sign that you need to turn and kick him hard and then run.

In Leviticus 19:13, the term *defraud* is used as part of the Old Testament law. There it is not speaking in a sexual way, but more in the way of selfishness. We are not to defraud another to get what we want.

In First Corinthians 6 we are warned that as Christians we are not to take a brother to court, to the point that we would even allow ourselves to be defrauded, before we would let the name of Christ be hurt. In other words, if a brother in Christ intentionally and deceitfully takes something from you, you would rather give it up than go to court and hurt the cause of Jesus Christ.

Proverbs chapters 6 and 7 talk about the strange woman who uses defrauding by her dress, by her fair speech, and by the batting of her eyes—she lures in the young man, and he comes in willingly. Ladies that flirt are practicing Proverbs 6 and 7—they are defrauding. They are offering something that really is not theirs to give, with no intention of fulfilling all that they promise.

Sinful

Third, not only does the term defraud in this context mean sly, selfish, but also sinful. We saw this in verse 6 where he says no man is to go beyond, to step over the boundaries. To defraud is to step over the boundaries that God has drawn on where a proper relationship should be. If you step over that line, it is sinful—trespassing over the line that God has drawn.

Maybe we should put up a sign over every young lady and young man in our church and say, "Trespassers will be prosecuted," because that is exactly what God says. You might think you can get away with it, but remember that God is the avengers of all those that are defrauded.

Beware—you have been warned. You step over this boundary and you are inviting God's prosecution in your life. You could step over this line and do it without anyone else knowing—but remember that God will know.

Sensual

Fourth, in verse 7 Paul talks about uncleanness, so defrauding is also sensual. God has not called us to uncleanness. This is not talking about physical involvement only, but also emotional involvement. It is impureness in thoughts and motives. It is fleshly desires that are outside the orders of God. And it leads to physical involvement.

Examples of Defrauding

Defrauding is seen when a young man or a young lady promises to someone else of the opposite sex a relationship that they have no right or ability to fulfill. "Let's get emotionally involved, let's get tied together, let's care about one another, and let's go steady—but after all, I am only 12 years old so we can't get married yet." You may laugh at that, but in our society it is promoted and acceptable in the world's views to have a boyfriend or girlfriend when you are that young, and even younger.

If a young man and young lady get in a relationship when they are not ready for marriage, it always leads to defrauding. It might just be a simple communication back and forth, until they get to the point where they begin to enjoy the company of one another. And my, aren't they dreamy? Isn't it wonderful?

It might step up another notch, and now they exchange love notes with one another, and let each other know that they care about each other. It might go all the way to physical involvement with one another. But anywhere along the way, defrauding is involved.

This sensual defrauding is not just reserved for unmarried people that are looking forward to being married one day. Men that are married and ladies that are married can do the same. They do so when they get involved with someone of the opposite sex, anytime a so-called affair takes place—God calls it adultery. That is defrauding. It is double defrauding, because it always involves defrauding the person that they are with, as well as the one that they are married to.

Someone says, "Well, I won't go that far. I would never get physically involved." But defrauding occurs when there is just an emotional bond with someone of the opposite sex that you are not married to. When you find yourself going to the office and you can't wait to be in the company of that certain lady—young or old—or can't wait to be in the company of that man—young or old—you are defrauding.

Your heart goes pitter-pat, your steps get a little quicker, you can't wait to see them and sit and talk with them. You think you have it all covered over but others where you work have noticed and are already beginning to whisper about it. "Why do they spend so much time together? Have you noticed how they look at each other?" Beware—inordinate affection, uncleanness, and defrauding are taking place.

Someone says, "But I haven't done anything wrong. I haven't touched her. We are just friends and enjoy each other's company." But the Bible says it is defrauding. You don't have to touch to be there. She does not belong to you.

How about single people? Anytime a young man and a young lady get into a close friendship, they are defrauding. You may say you are just friends, but everyone watching knows it is deeper than that. You are not just friends. You are close friends. You have moved from casual friendship to close friendship.

You enjoy being around each other, and you become close, and would prefer just sitting and talking to them instead of everyone else. When you go out with the rest of the young people that is exactly what you end up doing. The rest of the group knows not to talk to you because the two of you are locked in conversation. It is defrauding.

That is the definition of defrauding. And I can just hear some of you saying, "What is the harm? Don't you know that young people need to get to know each other? After all, what could go wrong? They are not touching. They are good kids—we trust them."

Let me just say that I don't trust any of my kids. And let me tell you—your kids are that bad too. There isn't a kid on this earth that you can trust.

Now, young people, before you stone me, let me tell you how I came to this conclusion. I was young once. I know how I acted, how the other guys acted, and how the girls acted. I know how young people act and I don't think they have gotten any better in this day and age. Unfortunately, my kids inherited my sin nature.

In the next chapter we want to look at the dangers that come with defrauding. Some people may think that it is not such a big deal. But let me warn you—God has a much different opinion!

Chapter Three
Dangers of Defrauding

So what are the dangers of defrauding? Let me just warn you right now that God takes this business of sensual and sexual sin seriously. The poster child in the Bible for this subject is David and Bathsheba. His lust of concupiscence turned into full-blown adultery, which turned into murder, which then turned into the judgment of God on his family.

David's son Amnon raped his sister Tamar, then his brother Absolem murdered his brother Amnon in retaliation for the rape. The kingdom was ripped apart and lives were lost. His closest friend and counselor in the palace turned on him because he was the grandfather of Bathsheba and could not let the bitterness go. Many lives were destroyed because of sensual lust that David could not control.

How does it all end up? We know that David wrote many of the Psalms in our Bible. Some of the Psalms are called Penitential or Psalms of Confession. Many of those were written around this time in David's life. They are full of mental and emotional and physical anguish that he went through because he violated God's principles about defrauding. It is that serious.

The Negative Commands of God

Some of the most serious consequences for sins in the Bible are reserved not for sins of omission, but for sins of commission, and specifically for those sins that are committed when we step over the bounds of the negative commands. God says, "Thou shalt not," and we disregard God's command and go ahead and do it anyway. God's greatest judgments are reserved for those kinds of sin.

Genesis chapter three

In Genesis chapter three God told Adam and Eve they could eat of all the trees in the Garden except for the Tree of the Knowledge of Good and Evil. God told them, "If you eat of that tree, you shall surely die." What happened? Eve was tempted and took of the fruit, she ate of it and gave to Adam, he ate of the fruit, and we are all affected because of their sin.

God gave them a negative command—do not eat of that tree—but they chose to break it and brought upon the human race the curse of Almighty God. Those are not small consequences, my friend.

First Kings chapter thirteen

In First Kings chapter thirteen, the man of God was sent out to talk to Jeroboam. He was to talk to Jeroboam, tell him of God's judgment, then turn and go home a different way. The man did what God told him to do. He went and preached a fiery message of judgment to Jeroboam, and then left to go back home.

On the way back home, 2 young men met him. Their father was a prophet of God and he sent his sons to tell the young prophet that he was to come to their house for dinner. So the young man went. Sadly, because he disobeyed, God sent a lion to kill him on his way home. My friend, if you disobey a negative command of God, you are in trouble.

Colossians 6:4

There is a command to fathers in Colossians 6:4, ***"Provoke not your children to wrath."*** Hmmm, what would happen if I broke this negative command from God? I would probably raise a rebel in my home.

Fathers, most often when you have troubles with your children in the home, it is because in the past you have provoked your child to wrath instead of dealing with them in a right way as God would have them to do.

Colossians 3:19

In Colossians 3:19 God commands to husbands concerning their wife is, ***"Be not bitter against them."*** Men, you better pay attention. I have seen it many times. When men get bitter towards their wives, it will destroy and tear up their marriage. It is a negative command that God is very, very serious about.

First Corinthians 7:3-5

In First Corinthians chapter seven, there is a command to both husbands and wives. It is not unusual for one or the other of them to break this command. God says,

"Let the husband render unto the wife due benevolence: and likewise also the wife unto the husband.

The wife hath not power of her own body, but the husband: and likewise also the husband hath not power of his own body, but the wife.

Defraud ye not one the other, except it be with consent for a time, that ye may give yourselves to fasting and prayer; and come together again, that Satan tempt you not for your incontinency." (First Corinthians 7:3-5)

Here is what God says. My body does not belong to me—it belongs to my wife. Therefore, if I take my body out and have sex with some other woman, I have defrauded my wife, because she owns me.

I don't own my body any more. I gave it to her when we were married. So I have not only defrauded the other woman but I have defrauded my wife. My body belongs to my wife and my wife's body belongs to me.

But what happens in the average marriage when husband and wife are upset with each other? They withdraw themselves and refuse to have sex with each other. God says that you are defrauding when you do that. You have broken one of God's negative commands and put your marriage in a place of great temptation and destruction. Many divorces have come about because of the violation of this command.

First Thessalonians 4:6

But the one we are looking at in this book is a negative command about getting to the marriage altar, and if violated by a man or a woman will also most likely set the stage for a divorce or at least some very serious problems in their marriage.

What are the dangers of me as a young person or old person getting involved with someone else when I cannot fulfill the expectations of the other person, which in this case would be marriage? Maybe I am too young, or I am already married, or I am not ready for marriage, but I am going to go ahead and get involved emotionally.

When I do that, I raise the expectations of the other person, even though I can't fulfill those expectations. God says that is defrauding. I am breaking a negative command from God—and I better be prepared for God's judgment in my life.

It happens a lot of times when young people decide to date each other to see if they are compatible. One party or the other begins to think, "Oh, this may be the one," but then the other person dumps them. Suicides have taken place because of that. It is a very dangerous game.

Five Dangers

As you study the scriptures, you find that there are many dangers to defrauding a brother or sister in Christ. But I want to specifically look at five dangers that we find in this passage in First Thessalonians.

You defraud your brother.

Number one: you defraud your brother. You cheat your brother. You are not going into the relationship thinking that you are there to help the other person. You are only concerned about yourself. You may lie to yourself and think you are helping them, but it is only a lie.

I could tell you stories of many people—even married men and women—that got involved with a member of the opposite sex with the idea, "I am going to help them spiritually." But their involvement draws them in further and further until their own marriage was destroyed and the lives of their children were destroyed also. It happens all the time.

Young lady, if that young man that you are interested in is not a Christian, you need to cut off that relationship immediately. Don't think that you are going to win him to Christ after you get married. He may make all kind of promises to you. He may even start attending church with you.

But beware—he is only doing it to win your affections. Once he has married you, he will go back to his own ways. I have seen many young ladies with broken hearts and broken marriages due to this problem.

God tells us to possess our own vessel in sanctification and honor. In other words, we need to control the passions of lust in our own self, not letting them rule and reign over us.

If I really care about this other person I am not going to lead them on or encourage them or somehow raise their expectations that I might be interested in them. If I do, I have defrauded them. Even if I have no intention of going any further, I have defrauded them.

You cross God's line.

Number two, when we defraud another person, we cross God's line. God was the one that drew the limit line in verse 6. He warns us that we are not to defraud a brother or sister in Christ.

Verse 7 tells us that God has not called us to uncleanness, to filthy thinking, to defrauding. He has called us instead to holiness, to holy thinking.

God has drawn the line for us and we have willfully crossed over that line. We have crossed over God's command. We have willfully violated God's Word saying, "I think I can do this. I don't think it will be that bad.

You challenge God's authority.

Number three, we challenge God's authority. You may think I am narrow minded, but I am the one that often winds up trying to help those that have violated God's commands and thought they could do it their own way. I would much rather you did things right the first time, instead of having to try to pick up the pieces when things fall apart.

When you decide to do things your own way, you are challenging God's authority. It is not me that you disagree with—this is God's Word. You are disagreeing with God.

Notice that God uses the word *despise* in verse 7. That means to *displace, to set aside, to reject, and to set at nought.* That is what it means when you despise God and His Word. That is a pretty serious charge.

You are calling for God's judgment.

Number four, you are calling for God's judgment. If you disregard God's command and go ahead and defraud your brother, you are asking God to judge you. In First Peter 5 God warns us that He resists the proud. But here God warns us that if we defraud another, He will bring vengeance on you. That is a step beyond.

I have been involved in Bible colleges for a lot of years during my ministry. I have seen student after student fall into immorality because of the sin of defrauding. Mentally in my mind, I can go through a list of many young men that were very promising—men that I thought might do a great work for God.

But every one of them that dipped their colors into this area of defrauding a young lady are either totally out of the ministry or "put on the shelf" and of no value to God. They ignored God's command and brought God's judgment into their life.

We have taken a strong stand in our church about the morals of any man—young or old—that we would dare to send out into the ministry. And it is for a good reason. I am of the number that believe a man in the ministry that steps into immorality should quit the ministry.

He can still serve and love God and find places of usefulness, but his ministry is done. That is narrow, but I think the office of a pastor is too serious to jeopardize it by such a sin.

It is foolish to pick a fight with another person, especially if he is bigger than you. But how much more foolish it is to raise your fists to God and ask Him to fight you. You don't have a chance. When you defraud, you are asking for God's judgment.

In Jude 7, God talks about how He destroyed Sodom and Gomorrah. He showed His vengeance against their sin—and God looks on defrauding in the very same light. You don't make the rules, society doesn't make the rules—God makes the rules.

It will corrupt your marriage.

Number five, it will corrupt your marriage. Here is how it will happen. The young man and young lady get involved in a relationship, and it later falls apart. One of two reactions will be normal for them.

Sometimes they will withdraw in the next relationship because they don't want to get hurt. If they eventually get married, they will withhold themselves from their husband or their wife and not be open with them—physically or emotionally. In most marriages where there are problems with openness, if you go back and check you will find that somewhere in a past relationship, they have been defrauded.

The other reaction that will be seen is anger. Once a person gets defrauded, they get angry and they turn loose in lewdness and immorality. In that approach, they end up abusing many others. I have seen both men and ladies that have had this reaction.

Defrauding will also corrupt the relationship between a husband and a wife, and will eventually destroy their marriage. If either one of them get caught up in a relationship with another person besides their spouse—whether emotionally or physically—it causes great harm and heartache.

Chapter Four
Deliverance from Defrauding

How do you get delivered from defrauding? If you are all caught up in the boyfriend/girlfriend dating scene, how to you break free from that and do things God's way instead?

The Pastor

It starts with a pastor. That is his job—to preach the Word of God and to warn you of the dangers of defrauding. I am passionate about this subject because I messed up, I have seen others mess up—and I have seen the right way in God's Word. So my job is to warn you and to show you the right way.

My job is not to get your approval, but God's approval. My job is to forewarn you and to plead with you to do it God's way. If you reject the Word of God, you are not despising me but you are despising God and His Word.

The Parents

Parents, you have the greatest responsibility in this matter. I can preach and teach the truths of God's Word, but unless you reinforce them in your home, your children will reject what they hear at church. If you go home and criticize the preacher and don't uphold the standards of the church, don't be surprised when your children rebel and walk away from the things of God.

Your children are under your care until they are married. They may not always live in your house, but they are still under your authority. You too must plead with them. As they get older, they can reject your counsel. But hopefully you have laid the foundation when they are young. Hopefully you have their heart and they will listen to you and be concerned about following your teachings.

Think about it this way. What would you do if your child was ready to walk out on a busy highway? If you are a normal parent, you would grab him and pull him back and warn him of the danger. You would be passionate about it. You are going to talk to them in such a way as to instill fear in them, because you don't want them to do it again.

In Colossians chapter 3, verse 5 God tells us, ***"Mortify therefore your members which are upon the earth; fornication, uncleanness, inordinate affection, evil concupiscence, and covetousness, which is idolatry."*** Remember we said that concupiscence is that a craving, an illicit desire that is outside the will of God. Don't let your kids live there.

It is not God's will for your young person to get into a relationship with someone that they cannot marry. What do you do in that situation? God tells us to put those desires to death. You can stab them or you can starve them.

Stab the lust

Here is an example of how to stab lustful cravings. Remember the story of the woman who declared her love to her preacher? The preacher said to the woman that had just declared her love for him, "Wait just a minute. I will be right back." He then went and found his wife and brought her to where the other woman was.

He then asked the other woman to tell his wife what she had told him. She didn't want to at first but he insisted and she finally did. Then he said, "Ladies, I believe in strong pastoral authority, but in this case, I think it is best for me to leave and let you two ladies handle this." He then walked away.

Now, let me ask you a question. Do you think that other woman ever told him again that she loved him? No, I doubt that she ever will.

What did that preacher do? He stabbed the lust—that inordinate affection—that this other woman had for him. He put it to death right then and there.

Parents, one of the best things you can do if your child gets involved in the boyfriend/girlfriend scene is to take action immediately. If there is a way that you can stab that lust and kill it immediately, then do it. When you see them standing and talking too long to someone of the opposite sex, don't be afraid to get between them and put a stop to it.

I am not talking about just casual conversation. You can tell if they are locked in conversation. Some parents would never do that—but if their child was standing on the highway about to get run over by a truck, they would be passionate about getting them out of danger. Do you think an 18-wheeler is worse than the judgment of God? I don't want the judgment of God on my kids.

Starve the lust

If they are already too far into the boyfriend/girlfriend scene, stabbing the lust may not work. In that case, you need to starve it. In Romans 4:19 and Hebrews 11:12, God uses this word mortify and in both cases it refers to Abraham's body being dead—not physically dead, but dead to the point that he can't have children any more unless God does a miracle in his life. What happened? Over a period of time, his body got old enough he could no longer father children.

Parents, if you remove the wrong influence from the life of your child, you can starve the inordinate affection and the evil concupiscence. You remove things like conversation—they don't talk anymore together. They stay with you at all times. They don't go to youth group activities or Sunday School class. They stay with you.

That is tough—but the alternative is losing your child. Do you want to settle for that option? It means no texting. If they can't control it, take the phone away from them. If they have pictures of the guy or girl, gifts from them, or notes from them, get rid of them. That is your job, Mom and Dad. Starve it—don't keep feeding it or it will never go away.

The People

This is referring specifically to the young man or the young lady that is involved in defrauding. What can you do? How can you get free from this sin so it is not destroying your life?

Stab it by not being involved in the boyfriend/girlfriend scene. Young ladies, don't stand around talking to young men. Young men, don't stand around talking with the young ladies, trying to impress them. When you do so, you open up your heart and your emotions to lustful thinking. If your heart is already involved, cut off all conversation with him/her.

As a man, I don't have trouble having casual conversations with the ladies of this church. But you won't find me off somewhere alone, locked in conversation with any of them. The ladies that work in the office don't find me back there with them chit-chatting all the time. I have purposed to guard my heart and guard my marriage. There is one woman I love—and I intend for it to stay that way. There is only one lady that God intended for me to have that kind of a relationship with.

If you find that your emotions are stirred by a certain young man or young lady, don't get around that person anymore. Cut off all conversations and texting. Cut your friends off if they encourage you to get back involved. Don't spend time thinking about them. Get rid of any mementos and gifts from them. There are many things that you can do to guard your heart.

You can be casual friends with those of the opposite sex, but you cannot be close friends. Anytime you find your heart drifting that way, it is a warning sign that you are getting too close. When you find yourself thinking about them all the time and wanting to be around them, you need to back it off. The wise young man and lady pay attention to those flutterings of emotions, and guards their heart.

Samson was a mighty man that God had intended to use. But his weakness for the opposite sex got him in trouble, and his life was ruined. Please don't think you can handle it. Satan knows your weakness as well.

The boyfriend/girlfriend scene is dangerous. It can destroy your future marriage and it can destroy your life. It will turn God into your enemy and it will destroy your ministry. It can potentially destroy many other lives. Please understand that there is a lot at stake.

Single life is the foundation for betrothed life. If you don't get single life right, you are not ready to move on to betrothal and then into marriage.

Chapter Five
The Three Stages of Life

There are basically three stages of life that God talks about in the Word of God—single, betrothed, and married. We want to look at each of these stages a little bit.

Single Life

The first stage is single life. That is how life starts and is a wonderful part of life. But somewhere during the teen years, a young man or a young lady starts getting interested in the opposite sex. And if you follow the way of the world and go the boyfriend/girlfriend route, all of a sudden your life got very complicated.

Purpose of single life

But that is not what God intended. The purpose of the single life according to God is found in First Corinthians 7:2—*to please the Lord.* So the one goal of a Christian single person should be to please the Lord in all you do.

If you can focus your attention on loving God, serving God, doing His will and doing what He says, then it cuts out all the emotional mess of the boyfriend/girlfriend scene. It will keep you from getting caught up in the emotional game of, "I have to have someone to love me." Knowing that God loves me and I love Him is good enough.

The single life is *also meant to be one of purpose*. Jesus is our example, and at the age of twelve we see Him sitting in the Temple—not with His peers, but with a group of older men who were doctors and lawyers. He was listening to them, getting their input, asking questions, and answering questions.

Your kids don't need other peers their age. That is the philosophy of the world. But God says that what your kids need is a relationship with Him and a relationship with Mom and Dad. The moment other kids step in and the peer influence starts becoming the most important thing in their life, they need to be pulled out of that situation until they can control their attitudes and their hearts.

That is the purpose of single life—*to learn how to control your emotions and how to guard your heart*. Jesus at the age of twelve was extremely mature. Your child is not perfect like Jesus was, but that is still the goal of single life.

During this stage, the young person will struggle with their emotions. They need to learn how to control their emotions and how to get along with others and how to serve others and help around the house.

Parents at this stage should be paying attention to how their child interact with others, how they deal with their brothers and sisters, how they deal with people in society, and how they treat those of the opposite sex as they get older. These things will tell you a lot about whether or not your son or daughter is ready for marriage.

Sometimes God chooses to leave a person in this single stage, and they never marry. If you say, "Oh, I don't want to stay in this stage," you are not ready to move beyond that stage. If you can't be content in the stage that God has placed you in, you are not ready to move on.

Many young people start the boyfriend/girlfriend cycle early in their teen years. They break up, and within a week they have another one. Another week or two, and they break up again. They can't stand living without someone.

They don't know what love is. They call it love, but it is really lust— the lust of concupiscence, a craving desire to have someone, to have a relationship with someone. It is like an addiction. They are not ready for marriage.

Betrothal Stage

The second stage is often ignored and certainly is not taught in most places. It is to be betrothed. Many people are afraid of that word, but it is a Bible word. Its purpose is found in Jeremiah 2:2 where it speaks of *"the love of thine espousals."*

God's design is that during the betrothal stage is when you learn to love that person you are going to marry. If you don't want to wait until that stage of your life, you are not ready to be married.

Betrothal does not sound practical to most people because they don't want to trust God. They want to date around and try this person and that person. In the process, they end up leaving a lot of used merchandise behind, hoping to find the right one.

Young man, when you are defrauding that young lady, you are also defrauding their future spouse. When you hurt her, you are setting the stage for her to withdraw from her future husband so she won't get hurt again. You may have very well set the stage for her future divorce.

You have also defrauded the young lady that you will someday marry. God's grace can heal these hurts—but why do you want to go through all the heartache? Wouldn't it be much better to do it God's way?

The Bible terms it as *"the love of thine espousals."* How often have I seen it! A young man and a young lady keep their hearts clean and pure, and they do things the right way. The young man asks the father for permission to marry his daughter, the young lady agrees and they become betrothed.

They have never spent time together alone with each other and they may have some worry about whether or not they can love each other. But give them a few weeks spending time together and I guarantee you the love will be there. It is the neatest thing that I have ever seen. And then they are absolutely worthless until they get married—and I love it! It is the way God intended it to be.

Purpose of Betrothal

Betrothal is for the purpose of blossoming love. The goal of the young man is to woo that young lady—to court her, to romance her, to think of ways to show love to her.

During this period, there is no physical involvement whatsoever—no kissing, no hugging, no intimacy there. It is an opening of the soul to the other person, and the other person opening their soul to you—and knowing that you love each other dearly and want to spend the rest of your lives together.

Young people, you have no business opening your soul like that to anyone of the opposite sex—with the exception of your parents—until you are betrothed to the one you are going to marry. That is the purpose of the betrothal period.

In the New Testament, the church is pictured as being betrothed to Jesus Christ. But the marriage supper does not take place until after the rapture. Therefore, it is during the betrothal period that we best can portray the picture of the love of Christ for His Church.

What does that love look like? Christ loved the church and gave Himself for it. The young man that is betrothed to a young lady should love her, no matter what she reveals to him. He loves her and is committed to marry her.

A Biblical example of betrothal is seen in the life of Joseph and Mary. Joseph was betrothed to Mary when he found out she was expecting a child. What did he do? He did not put her away, but he loved her and was committed to her. God blessed his life because of that commitment to Mary.

That is what love is all about. Love doesn't say, "Let's dismiss each other because of these problems." Love say, "Let's work through the problems because we have a commitment here." That is what betrothal is all about.

Betrothal is very different than dating. The dating scene really builds lying and deceiving into your relationship. You don't know if you can tell the other person the truth about yourself. If you tell them the truth, they may not like you anymore. They will end the relationship.

Betrothal life is meant to be one where the young man and young lady are so in love with each other because they have already made the commitment to be married. There is no fear of being honest with each other but a mutual sharing of their heart and soul with one another.

They build a bond with each other. They are both very excited and happy with eyes only for each other. It is a wonderful thing to watch, because you know it is a genuine love that will give them a wonderful start in their marriage.

The word *betrothed* is found twelve times in the New Testament and the word espoused is used seven times, for a total of nineteen times. The word *marriage* is used eighteen times in the New Testament. This tells me that preaching on betrothal is just as important as preaching about marriage. But in the average church of today, you will never hear it preached or taught.

Here is why it is so important and should be preached. Single life is the foundation for betrothed life. If you don't get single life right, you are not ready to move on to betrothal and then into marriage.

What a difference it would make in marriages if young people would evaluate the character of that single person they are interested in to see if they are ready to move on to betrothal.

Married Stage

Betrothal moves on to the next stage which is married life. This is meant to be a time of service, when two people serve together as one. In marriage, you set aside your own selfish purposes for the good of the marriage. If you are both committed to each other and to the Lord, your marriage will stand the tests and trials of time. In the home, the goal is to serve others and Christ, not self.

We will look a little more at these three stages as we go along. But first we want to look at our culture and the different ways that people get to the marriage altar.

Chapter Six
Evaluating the Culture

Introduction

There are a lot of things in our culture that are good. But there are also a lot of thing that we cannot accept as Christians. In First John 2, God tells us that we are not to love the world. He is talking about is the world system—the way the world operates.

For example, if you were to go out on the street and ask the average person walking down the sidewalk, "How do you think this world got here?" most people would tell you the world came about by evolution—by a big bang. That is what the world is taught. If you ask them why they believe that, they would say, "That is what science teaches us."

If you have done any study at all, you know that there are a number of scientists that have serious problems with the whole subject of evolution. And yet the way the scientific community is ruled today, if you have questions about evolution, you will very probably lose your job, your grants and funding. Therefore many of them choose to keep their mouths closed because they are afraid.

I can understand that. But as a Christian, I can't accept the belief of the world. I read my Bible and see what God says. The Bible teaches clearly that God created the world in six literal days, and God rested on the seventh day. I can't be influenced by the thinking of the world. I need to stand on what God says.

Generally if we look at any issue that we face today—fashion, music, science—how do we as Christians generally set our standard? Most of the time, we look at where the world is, and we set our standard a little bit to the right. However, if we go back fifty years, the things that are accepted today were looked on as wrong then, even by the world.

When we buy our standards from the way the world thinks, we are not going to be looking at things in a right way. In fact, we are going to find ourselves loving the world. We need to set our standards according to the Word of God.

Many people get upset when you say that dating is wrong. If you are caught up in the way of the world, the things of God are going to seem strange to you. You are not going to like them. But even people in our world can recognize the dangers of the way those in the world get to the marriage altar.

As Christians, we need to remember that God has the answer to every question of life in the Word of God. We just need to find out what He has said. The subject of marriage is no different.

Genesis 2:18-25

"And the LORD God said, It is not good that the man should be alone; I will make him an help meet for him.

And out of the ground the LORD God formed every beast of the field, and every fowl of the air; and brought them unto Adam to see what he would call them: and whatsoever Adam called every living creature, that was the name thereof.

And Adam gave names to all cattle, and to the fowl of the air, and to every beast of the field; but for Adam there was not found an help meet for him.

And the LORD God caused a deep sleep to fall upon Adam, and he slept: and he took one of his ribs, and closed up the flesh instead thereof;

And the rib, which the LORD God had taken from man, made he a woman, and brought her unto the man.

And Adam said, This is now bone of my bones, and flesh of my flesh: she shall be called Woman, because she was taken out of Man.

Therefore shall a man leave his father and his mother, and shall cleave unto his wife: and they shall be one flesh.

And they were both naked, the man and his wife, and were not ashamed."

Marriage invented by God

Adam and Eve were the first man and wife that ever got married. God is the one that invented marriage. It wasn't that man figured it out and thought it would be a good idea. It was given by God.

When we consider marriage, we recognize that the state has something to do with a person's marriage legally. But there is so much more involved to a marriage than just getting a license and saying we have been married. There is also a spiritual commitment that ought to go along with that marriage.

In a world where divorces are mounting drastically and our society is being ripped apart at the seams, you and I as God's people ought to be very concerned about what is wrong at the base of everything. Some people just want to go put a band-aid on it and figure that will fix the problem. However, I think the problem starts long before the marriage even begins.

Getting to the Marriage Altar

The problem starts back in the days of making preparation for that marriage. And how we get to the marriage altar is important. If we follow the way of our culture, we will end up in the same mess that other people are in. We need to find out what God says. How should a Christian get to the marriage altar?

In Genesis 2:24 God says that a man should leave his father and mother and cleave to his wife. Have you ever thought that through?

When God gives this command to Adam, there are no fathers or mothers. There has never been a child born. So why did God say that?

I think part of the reason is because God wanted to establish the right order before the children were born, so that they were raised with the right understanding and the parents had the right understanding. God is the one who invented this original love story in getting Adam and Eve to this marriage altar so that they could get married to each other. God is already setting the stage for how their children are going to get to the marriage altar, even before they have been born.

Setting Standards

How does our culture set its standards? They ask, "How is everybody else doing it in society? What did your parents do? Your neighbors, your teacher, your friends—how do they normally do things?" That is the culture.

As Christians we cannot follow the way of our culture all the time. Everything in our culture is not wrong. But everything in our culture should be examined with the Word of God. "What does God say?"

That has changed a lot of things for me. There is some music that I enjoy, but I don't listen to it, because God has taught me better. Even though it is acceptable in the culture, it is not acceptable with God. Even though I was raised with that kind of music and my body enjoys listening to it, God has shown me that it is not good for me.

When we look at the issue of divorce, the world says that it is OK. In our culture, it is socially acceptable to be divorced. Many of you have gone through divorce, or your parents have gone through divorce.

Anyone who has had a divorce will tell you that it is a horrible experience. But it is part of our society and our culture. However, as Christians we shouldn't be accepting the standard of what society believes or does, but look at what God says about it. I realize that sin gets in the middle and messes things up and things get extremely complicated.

But when everything is said and done, we need to come back and say, "I am going to evaluate what I am going to do, not based on what the culture says, but on what God says. I need to get my life in line with God's Word instead of trying to twist God's Word to fit in with my culture's idea."

God has much to say in the Word of God about what a marriage is, and about how to get to the marriage altar. The most important decision that you and I will ever make in life, apart from salvation and our relationship with Jesus Christ, is the decision of who to marry. Therefore, we need to know what God says about this issue.

We can change jobs like we change shirts. We can change cars or houses every year. But when we come to marriage, it is meant to be something is permanent, so we better make sure that the choice we make of who to marry is the very best choice we could possibly make.

When I married my wife, it was with the view that this was for the rest of my life. Now, I have to tell you, my views on marriage were not as strong when I got married as they are today. I have a much more narrow view now than I had before about the permanence of marriage and the importance of choosing the right marriage partner.

My views have not grown because marriage is so easy, but because marriage is so important. I have performed many marriages over the years and given counsel to many married couples. I have seen the consequences of wrong choices.

I am convinced that the way we get to the marriage altar has a major impact in how the marriage progresses and whether or not it will last or will end in divorce. So why do we throw our kids out into the world to figure out who they are going to marry and how they are going to get married? Why do we send them to go talk to their friends to figure out it all out?

Generally in the world, the way a girl decides whether she likes a guy is whether he is popular and handsome and on the football team. On the other hand, the guys look for whether or not a girl is popular, whether she is pretty, and if she is a cheerleader. Those are some pretty non-essential external things to look at.

Often they have no clue of what is really important to look for in a marriage partner. Why would we just let our kids find their own way in this very important subject? They need our guidance. They need to be taught what God says about how to get to the marriage altar in a right way.

It is not unusual in American culture today for a girl to bring their future spouse home and say, "His name is Fred. See my ring. We are getting married." And the parents haven't even met her fiancé. I don't believe that is the way that God designed it to be. There are some things that we need to change.

Chapter Seven
Four Ways of Getting to the Marriage Altar

In our culture, there are basically four different ways that a person can get to the marriage altar. We want to look at each of those four ways and look at some characteristics of each one.

Dating

The first way, and the most popular in America today would be what we call dating. Dating is a *temporary relationship that focuses on recreational romance*. Guy meets girl, they like each other, go out on a date, maybe one time, maybe more, then they break up and never see each other again.

No big deal, right. The guy decided that she wasn't the kind of girl he wanted, so he went on down the road. But the girl feels rejected. She thinks, "I must not have dressed right, or fixed my hair right, or said the right things." Somehow she didn't impress him enough to stay around, so she is going to be all worried, and try harder with the next guy.

That is a dating relationship. It is a temporary relationship that focuses on recreational romance. It doesn't matter what age they are—six, twelve, eighteen, twenty-five or forty—it is recreational romance. They go out to enjoy each other's company.

The guy is in a romantic relationship with the girl for one reason—is he enjoying it? If he stops enjoying it, he is gone. Or when the girl gets tired of the guy, she says good-bye and goes looking for another guy that will keep her happy. Recreational romance—does it please me? That is dating.

Dating can have parental involvement. Mom and dad sometimes will even say, "Bring the boy in here and we want to talk to him before you go out with him." That is far better than just letting her go out and find her own guy.

But at the same time, the whole idea of just turning them out and letting them hunt and peck and figure out who they are going to marry all on their own I think is really deadly and destructive. You are deluded if you think you can ever fit that into a Bible pattern of how to get to a marriage.

God prepared Eve for Adam and put the two together. Adam didn't need five girls to choose from. Eve didn't need five guys to choose from. God paired them up and put them together, and it worked just fine.

So dating is recreational romance that focuses on making me happy. It needs no parental involvement, although sometimes parents are involved. And then it might end in marriage, but really marriage doesn't even have to be the end goal.

Case in point—two six year olds dating. Do you think they will be married in the next six months? No, that is ridiculous because they are not old enough or ready to get married. But it happens in our culture, and when it happens, there are multitudes of adults that will look and smile and say, "Isn't that cute?"

No, it is not cute. It is dangerous, because dating is practice for divorce. We are learning how to break up, not stay together. And if it eventually leads to marriage, there is always the option of divorce if it doesn't work out. After all, look at all the break-ups they survived before they finally got married. Another break-up is no big deal.

Arranged Marriage

The second way which is way on the other side of the spectrum is arranged marriage. We don't see much of this in America, but with the influx of Muslims, it has become more prevalent.

In arranged marriages the parents on both sides choose the spouse, and they have never even laid eyes on each other until they get to the marriage altar. The boy and the girl have no say in the matter, and are just presented their spouse when they arrive to be married.

Arranged marriages are not what God intended. They are not wise neither are they Biblical. They don't fit into the scriptural pattern. If I am going to choose how to get to the marriage altar, it is not going to be dating or an arranged marriage. Neither one fits the Bible pattern at all.

Courtship

There is a third method of getting to the marriage altar that is called courtship. This method has come about in our day and age, and it is rather popular among homeschoolers and in Christian circles.

As Christian people noticed that the dating scene was not wise, they decided to come up with a better plan of girls and guys getting to know each other. I think it is much better than dating, but there are still some problems with it.

Courtship is *a serious temporary relationship*. In courtship technically, a boy and a girl never go to courting until both of them and their parents have determined that they are ready to get married, and they are now looking for their spouse. So they are not getting together with the idea of just having fun, but rather they are actually looking for the right one. They are looking for someone to marry.

But courting is temporary, because there is no commitment. The young man goes to ask permission from the father to court his daughter. The young man meets with the young lady a few times and then eventually he says yea or nay, and she says yea or nay. They are making decisions on whether they want to marry each other or not.

But in the middle of all of this, one of the things that is taking place is that he has to woo her and win her heart. So he needs to bring her flowers and chocolates, and do all those romantic things. He is trying to impress her and get her to say yes.

So courtship becomes a serious temporary relationship. There is no commitment in that either party can back out either time they want. Also the parents have the option of breaking it off at any time. It is a temporary relationship which focuses on marriage, which makes it better than dating.

But at the same time, it is focused on winning the heart of the other person—and that is where the problem comes in. If my heart doesn't go pitter-patter, then I am going to dump them and go looking for another. It often ends up in break ups.

That is the reason that many of the homeschoolers and other Christians are beginning to reject courtship. They have seen the great damage done to the numbers of young ladies and young men who have gotten involved in a courting relationship only to be dumped. Broken hearts are the end result.

Something is wrong in the culture of courting. But let me say if I had to choose between these three, I would go for courting hands down. It is much better than the other two, but there are still some problems with it. There is something better, and that is what God teaches in His word.

Betrothal

The fourth way is what the Bible calls betrothal or espousal. Please note the difference. Betrothal is NOT an arranged marriage. Some people try to define it that way, but that is absolutely wrong. That may be how some people practice it, but it is wrong.

I have seen other people practice courtship but they are practicing it like betrothal in the Bible. The name you use is not the big issue here. It is the Bible principles behind it that are either being followed or being violated—that is what is important.

Betrothal is a committed relationship, a serious permanent relationship. The difference between it and courtship is that courtship is only temporary. In courtship you are deciding whether to back out or stay in the relationship. In betrothal, you step into the relationship and you have already made up your mind that God intends for you to marry the person.

So it is a permanent relationship from the start. The commitment has already been made. The young man and the young lady know they are headed to the marriage altar. That is betrothal.

It is *a serious permanent relationship that focuses on marriage preparedness.* The whole betrothal period should be less than a year. During this time, it is a preparing time for marriage—not a physical involvement time but a preparation of the emotions to fall in love with one another. It is a time of learning about the other person, to want to meet their needs, to prepare and establish communication lines so that when they get married they know how to communicate. That is the goal in this period of time.

It is *a serious permanent relationship that focuses on marriage preparedness and also on cultivating a romantic involvement.* There is nothing wrong with them showing that they love each other. In fact, they need to be doing that—but always apart from physical contact.

They don't belong kissing or holding hands or hugging, but they need to find ways to express love apart from physical involvement. That means speaking the words to each other. That means showing your love by bringing gifts or by acts of service.

This involvement and this process happens under parental supervision, but only after there is a commitment to go all the way to the marriage altar.

Which way do I choose?

Those are the 4 ways in our culture to get to the marriage altar. Let me just say, I don't care if you try to do betrothal or courtship, you are not going to follow everything just perfectly so. Each individual case is different and there will be some adjustments along the way.

I am of the opinion that betrothal is the closest to the Biblical model. But I am not going to suggest to you that getting to betrothal is an easy thing. There are some real difficulties—but there are also some answers if we look at betrothal with the attitude that you want to do it God's way.

Of course, the most important thing that we should consider as a Christian is what God says about any matter. The issue of marriage is no different. God does have the answer in His Word.

Chapter Eight
What is the perspective of the Word of God?

Let's go to the perspective of God's Word for a moment. Ultimately, the method that we choose needs to be evaluated according to God's Word. I have given you four methods that people use to get to the marriage altar in our culture—but which is right and which is wrong?

Or is it like some people say—just take whichever one you like? It is your choice. But I believe that our choices should be governed by the Bible pattern and Bible principles. So we want to look for a little bit about the Bible pattern or the Bible perspective.

Three Stages of Life

There are 3 distinct stages of life. We talked a little bit about this already. All of us begin our life single. There has never been anyone born married. Then single life moves Biblically into betrothal or espousal. Then that moves into married life.

That is the ideal Biblical pattern. I realize that for many of us, we didn't follow this pattern because we were not taught it or didn't understand it. However, that doesn't release me from the requirement of a proper kind of a marriage, or shirking my parental responsibility.

I want my children to be taught right. Just because I didn't know the truth doesn't mean my kids can't have the truth. I want to teach them right and help to direct their steps. I want to do all I can to guide their steps. I want their marriage relationship to be all that God wants it to be. That is my goal with my children and my grandchildren.

Why Dating is Unbiblical

Single life is the foundation of your life. The Bible is very clear that single life is not meant to be a time of physical intimacy with people of the opposite sex. There is no excuse or place for physical intimacy in single life. The hormones say, "Let's do it," but God says that it is fornication and it is wrong.

God says in First Corinthians 7 that it is good for a man not to touch a woman. The context there is speaking about when you are in a single state. You have no business touching another person in any sexual manner. Nowhere in the Bible does scripture talk about dating or courtship or arranged marriages. The only model found in the Bible is betrothal.

"Now concerning the things whereof ye wrote unto me: It is good for a man not to touch a woman.

Nevertheless, to avoid fornication, let every man have his own wife, and let every woman have her own husband.

Let the husband render unto the wife due benevolence: and likewise also the wife unto the husband.

The wife hath not power of her own body, but the husband: and likewise also the husband hath not power of his own body, but the wife.

Defraud ye not one the other, except it be with consent for a time, that ye may give yourselves to fasting and prayer; and come together again, that Satan tempt you not for your incontinency.

But I speak this by permission, and not of commandment.

For I would that all men were even as I myself. But every man hath his proper gift of God, one after this manner, and another after that.

I say therefore to the unmarried and widows, It is good for them if they abide even as I.

But if they cannot contain, let them marry: for it is better to marry than to burn." (First Corinthians 7:1-9)

Husbands and wives have a responsibility one to another to meet the physical needs of each other. But that is at the married state, not at the single or betrothed state. Husband and wives ought not to deny one another in physical intimacy. There ought to be a meeting of the needs of the other person.

Paul said that he wished that all men were like him. How was Paul? At this point, he was single. Paul says that single life is good. There is nothing wrong with being single.

Preparation for Divorce

Here is what happens a lot of times in our culture. The moment young people graduate from high school, they think they have to go hunting for a mate. Let me just tell you, there are worse things than not getting married—like getting into a marriage when you are not ready or getting into a marriage where there is one fight after another.

If you go running into the wrong kind of a marriage that is what is going to happen. If you don't know what to look for or where to look, you are liable to wind up in a marriage that will mess you up.

I thank God that even though my wife and I didn't know what we were doing, God pulled it together into something beautiful. But there are plenty of people on the other side that can testify that they didn't know what they were doing and they got into a royal mess because they didn't do things right to start with.

Dating is nothing more than preparation for divorce. It is not wonder that when two people get married, it isn't long down the road they are ready to cut and run. During their dating life, they have learned that you get into a relationship and when it doesn't work you go down the road. They haven't learned that commitment in supposed to be in a marriage relationship.

Single life is not designed to be a time of testing your emotions with the opposite sex. That is to be reserved for marriage. The purpose of single life is that we might give ourselves to the Lord, totally and completely.

I have watched youth groups destroyed by the dating mentality. I have watched young people in colleges destroyed by the dating mentality. Why am I so against dating? Because I have watched too many lives destroyed.

I have watched as a college professor, as a pastor, as a friend, and I say there has got to be a better way. We need to find God's way in all of this.

Several years ago I talked to a young man that was telling me about how hard single life was. Then he got engaged, and he came to see me and tell how hard engaged life was. He thought it would be better when he got married.

I told him in a nice way that he was really rather dumb! Then I let him in on the secret that when he got married, it would get much worse. He got married, and he dropped out of school. He learned the hard way.

He had never learned in single life how to serve God and how to order his priorities. Single life is a preparation time and some people should never go beyond single life. They should stay single and thank God for the opportunity to serve.

Don't Get in a Hurry

The average age of marriage in America is 28 years of age. So young people, don't get in a hurry. Don't think you are going to be an old maid just because you are 18 and don't have a boyfriend yet. You are better off with no marriage than a wrong marriage.

Why am I against dating? If you get into dating, it puts your emotions in motion. All of a sudden, you are being controlled by your emotions. You walk in a room of other young people and as a young man, all you can see are the girls. You start checking them out and looking for the possibilities.

Or when you get finally paired off, everyone else in the room knows exactly who you are paired off with. I know how it goes. You say, "Oh, we're not a couple; we aren't paired off; we are not dating. We don't believe in that. We are just friends." But everyone else in the room knows that they are not allowed to talk to you because you are taken. If the other girls talk to you, that one certain girl will get mad.

Let me just tell you—that is not what we are about in our youth group at this church. If you know someone involved in the dating scene, they are not welcome to act that way here. And if they do act that way, we will talk to them. That is not what we want to promote. We do not want the dating spirit to wreck and ruin our youth group.

The goal in the single life is that the emotions be set on God and not on other people in a romantic relationship.

If you haven't learned how to control your emotions, you are not ready to be married.

Chapter Nine
God's Will in Each Stage of Life

Focus in Single Life: to Please God

In the single life, the focus needs to be on pleasing God. That is important because if you can learn how to please God and love Him with all your heart in your single life, you will be able to keep your heart set on God when you get married. The goal in single life is to learn to control your emotions and love God with all your heart, instead of being drawing into the dating scene.

But if you are all about finding somebody that makes you feel good and somebody that you like, the day will come when your feelings change. You may think you love them now and they make your heart go pitter-patter, but the day is going to come in marriage when you are going to wake up and say, "You know, the romantic feelings aren't there anymore."

I have been married now almost 40 years, and there are some days when I am right up at the top, excited, loving my wife with every fiber of my being. But there are other days when I am at the bottom, way low, and the romantic feelings are not there. Let me tell you—it is not my wife's fault.

If you have been married any length of time, you know that there are ups and downs in marriage. When your emotions are down low, it is not time to go looking for someone else. It is time to get control of your emotions and set your affections on the one you married and the one you love.

In Colossians 3:2 God tells us, *"Set your affections on things above, not on things on the earth."* The goal in the single life is that the emotions be set on God and not on other people in a romantic relationship. If you haven't learned how to control your emotions, you are not ready to be married.

If you are still fighting with those romantic emotions that come, and still trying to get control of them, then you need more training. In the meantime, you need to be kept away from the opposite sex until you can get control of yourself. You are not an animal—you are a person in whom the Spirit of God desires to dwell and control.

Focus in the Betrothal Period: Blossoming of Love

The shortest period of all of life should be the betrothal period. Single life is going to vary with every person, depending on how old you are when you enter the betrothal period.

The betrothal period should be around a year of time. Theoretically, if you live out a normal life, your married life is going to be longer than both of the first two stages.

The betrothal period is not a period of physical intimacy. It is meant to be a time of emotional intimacy and learning to be able to talk with one another. During this time, the young couple learn how to communicate with one another, and learn how to work through issues in life.

It is a preparation time for the marriage. It is a covenant—an agreement that we are going to get married. There is no fear on either side that something will happen and the marriage will be called off. They are committed to going all the way to the marriage altar.

A betrothal is a commitment that says, "No matter what, we are getting married. We are going to work through our difficulties." Now instead of the girl trying to impress the guy and win him over—and instead of the guy trying to impress the girl and fool her about what he is really like—they can both be honest with each other. Instead of trying to lie to one another, they can share their hearts with one another.

Does it always work? No, because people are sinners. But let me tell you. It is far better to do it God's way and be committed to each other and committed to working out the difficulties.

Yes, there will be differences of opinions between the young man and the young lady, and the betrothal time is the time to talk through these differences. That is what betrothal is meant to be.

The betrothal period is a binding together of hearts and a building of love for each other. The young man and the young lady look for ways to show their love to each other. It is very appropriate for them to say, "I love you." But it is not appropriate to say that when they are in the single stage.

Betrothal is a preparing for the marriage. Here is maybe the best way to put it. You have heard people say, "You ought to marry the love of your life. Marry the person you love." Betrothal turns that one its head, and says, "You need to love the person you marry."

That says the most about our view as God's people about what love in marriage is supposed to be all about. Love is not an emotion. Now, I want to feel like loving my wife. I want to enjoy that emotion and I want to work towards that all the time.

But I also know that I am not always going to get up and feel that way. I want my wife to know that I am committed to her, whether I feel like it or not. I am going to love her, no matter what, whether the feelings come or go.

I want to have the same commitment from her. If she had married me because she feels like it, when the feelings go, she might not want to be married to me.

I don't want her to be committed to me because she feels like it, because I know there will be days when she doesn't feel like it. I want her to be committed to me because she has made a commitment, whether the feelings are there or not.

The only way we can know that is possible from each other before marriage is to observe each other's life and see whether or not we are able to control our emotions before marriage ever takes place.

If you marry a man or woman who is run by their feelings and their emotions, you are stacking the deck against yourself that your marriage may just have really rocky times and may end in divorce.

Focus in the Marriage Period: to Please Each Other

What is the purpose of marriage? In First Corinthians 7:33-34, the Bible says *" But he that is married careth for the things that are of the world, how he may please his wife. There is a difference also between a wife and a virgin...she that is married careth for the things of the world, how she may please her husband."*

Let me first mention that when Paul is talking about caring for the things of the world, he does not mean it in a bad way. He is just saying that when you are married, there are responsibilities that you have to carry out that are not there when you are single.

For a man these responsibilities include caring for his wife, meeting her needs, providing a house for her to live in, etc. For the wife these repsonsiblities include cooking, cleaning, grocery shopping, caring for the children, etc.

All these things are done so that the husband pleases his wife, and the wife pleases her husband. In marriage, there is an addition of these duties that are not there when you are single.

When you are single, you have the opportunity to love God alone, without all the entanglements of the opposite sex. When you get married, there is one lady that you love, and she loves you. You are to please each other.

It doesn't matter what all the other women in the world think about you, as long as your wife loves you. That is where you need to put your attention.

But that attention comes in married life after I have learned how to put God first in single life. When I have learned to put God first in single life, then I add the extra weight of also caring for a wife when I get married. Then as time goes along, children will be added to that marriage, and I will be bearing more of a load.

There are changes and seasons in a marriage that you go through. As you move through all those seasons, your first commitment needs to be to the Lord, the second commitment needs to be to your spouse, and then to your children. If you turn that around, you will always have trouble in a marriage.

Parents, you need to pay attention here, because this is a big problem in many homes. Many husbands and wives let the kids come before their spouse. It causes instability in the home and eventually it will give major repercussions in your children's lives, and insecurity.

The only way to build security in those children is if mom and dad have a secure relationship with each other. The children need to know that you love each other. But it all starts with single life.

Why Betrothal is Biblical

If we are going to evaluate this God's way, we need to ask, "What is the best way to get to the marriage altar that would most please the Lord?" I don't think anyone can argue that either a dating relationship or an arranged marriage could fulfill that.

An arranged marriage is basically Mom and Dad controlling the young man and young lady. They are not ready to handle life on their own because their parents have handled their life up to that point.

Courtship at least is a little better, but it still leaves a lot of doors open for real destruction in the relationship. The ultimate goal should be betrothal and to try to follow the Bible principles that we will look at in the next few chapters. God does have some principles that are very clear in his word about how to get to the marriage altar.

A Picture of the Rapture

I want to look at a beautiful analogy. In the book of Ephesians chapter five, the Lord's church is compared to the Bride of Christ in a betrothal state. Jesus is not physically present with us right now. We don't see Him here. But one day He is coming back to get us.

Until then, we are in this betrothal state. Our goal should be to set our heart and our affections on the One that we love (Colossians 3:2), the One that is coming back for us. Most of us let our feelings run our life. We need to be taking control of our feelings and our emotions and not let them control us.

We are in a training time, a rehearsal period until Jesus comes. And the Lord is trying to get us to get our eyes off of everybody else and onto Him. What would you think if you were betrothed to some young lady and she kept going out to dinner with some other guy? Would it bother you a little bit? It would bother me a whole lot.

That is exactly what we do in our relationship with the Lord. We say, "I belong to Jesus and I want to be with Him, but there are other things that are more important right now. I am going to have to put the Lord off to the side. I can't be in church—I have to go make money." What we are really saying is that the Lord is not the most important one in our life.

Now here is where it gets really exciting! First Thessalonians chapter four says that one day Jesus will descend with a shout and we shall be caught up together to meet Him in the air. Why is that exciting? The rapture is a picture of the end of the betrothal period as the young man would come for his bride.

In Bible times, a young man would choose a young lady based on her character, and say, "She is the one I want to marry." He would go to his parents, and then he and his parents would approach the parents of the young lady and discuss with them the potential.

They would determine whether or not this young man was marriageable material or not. If they were satisfied, they would go to their daughter and ask her if she was willing. She made her determination, and said yea or nay.

If all 4 parties were in agreement—young man, young lady, and both sets of parents—then the father of the girl would give permission for the young man to marry his daughter, and the betrothal period began. The young lady would begin to sew her wedding dress, and prepare herself. She would put her coins in her headpiece and prepare her dowry. She was getting ready.

During this time, the young man paid the bride price to the father of the young girl. It was a gift to show the father how much he cares about this young lady. He built a house and prepared to take care of her, and provide for her financially. In other word, he needed to be stable.

The father of the girl had already given permission, but he didn't set the date of the wedding. It was the responsibility of the young man to determine when the wedding was to be. The young lady did not know when the date was, but she was ready and waiting.

One evening the young man would decide it was time for the wedding, but the young lady still would not know. He would get his friends together and they would go singing and playing instruments down the street, headed to the young lady's house. She would be waiting there with her bridesmaids, waiting for the bridegroom to come.

When the bridegroom got to her house, he would call for his betrothed, and she would go out to meet him. Then away they would go to the wedding celebration. I am not suggesting that we have to practice it that way today, but that is how it was in Bible days.

And that is what makes First Thessalonians 4 so special. We belong to the Lord. We are in a betrothal state right now, setting our affections on the Lord. One day, we don't know when, He is going to descend from heaven with a shout. He is looking for us to be ready in that day when He comes with a shout. We are to be ready to go, and so shall we ever be with the Lord.

For the child of God that loves Jesus, it will be a wonderful day. Our hearts are set where they ought to be, and we are ready at a moment's notice. I am ready to go and leave it all behind, because my heart is set on Him.

That is the picture of the young lady as she is at home. Whatever she is doing, when she hears her bridegroom coming, she drops it all and goes to meet him.

The way of the world to get to the marriage altar does not work. God does have a better way. Let's dare to find it and to practice it.

Chapter Ten
Three Bible Principles: Principle Number One

We have looked at four different ways that people in our culture get to the marriage altar. We now want to look at three Bible principles that we can use to evaluate which of these ways is best. These Bible principles cannot be violated without putting yourself in harm's way and putting yourself in great danger in your relationships with the opposite sex.

These three principles ought to be followed and can be used to examine your practice and the pattern that you follow to get to the marriage altar. Does it meet these three Bible principles?

Genesis 2:18-24

Almost everything in the Word of God can be found in seed form in the book of Genesis. It is where we start with almost everything we have in the world—sin, salvation, the Messiah, and murder. Getting to the marriage altar is no different. We find the first marriage in Genesis chapter two.

"And the LORD God said, It is not good that the man should be alone; I will make him an help meet for him.

And out of the ground the LORD God formed every beast of the field, and every fowl of the air; and brought them unto Adam to see what he would call them: and whatsoever Adam called every living creature, that was the name thereof.

And Adam gave names to all cattle, and to the fowl of the air, and to every beast of the field; but for Adam there was not found an help meet for him.

And the LORD God caused a deep sleep to fall upon Adam, and he slept: and he took one of his ribs, and closed up the flesh instead thereof;

And the rib, which the LORD God had taken from man, made he a woman, and brought her unto the man.

And Adam said, This is now bone of my bones, and flesh of my flesh: she shall be called Woman, because she was taken out of man.

 Therefore shall a man leave his father and his mother, and shall cleave unto his wife: and they shall be one flesh." (Genesis 2:18-24)

The principles or teachings of God's Word are very important. How you enact them or practice them in your life is also important. If you follow God's principles and get to the marriage altar God's way, it will save you a lot of trouble and heartache.

The opposite is also true. If you ignore God's principles and get the marriage altar in whatever way pleases you, it will cause you much trouble and much heartache. You can't ignore the Word of God and not have problems in your life.

I think that any of us that are already married can look back and see things we did wrong. When we compare what God says to our own practice, we can see where we messed up. We can see how God's principles would have safeguarded up and kept us from getting involved in things we are not proud of.

God does not give us His Word because He wants to restrict us and make our life miserable. He gave us guidelines in the Bible because He knows we can't figure things out on our own. If we will listen to what He has to say, it can really safeguard our life. God's way is definitely always best.

I want to look at these three principles that God gives us in His Word about getting to the marriage altar. Each one will be in the form of a question. These principles will help us to determine the best way for us to get to the marriage altar and be pleasing to God.

Principle Number One:
Have you reserved romance for a committed relationship?

Marriage is to be a committed relationship, and romance is to be saved for only that committed relationship. God never intended that you go around romancing all the women in the world. That is easy to figure out—just ask your wife, "Do you mind if I fall in love with another lady?" I am sure her reaction will let you know the truth!

And why can't you do it before you get married? Because that person you are romancing will eventually marry someone else. And eventually you will have to tell your wife, "I loved another one first." It is a detriment to your marriage relationship. God did not intend it at all.

Only need one wife

In Genesis 2:20 Adam named the animals, but he couldn't find a helpmeet for himself. The animals did not qualify. In verse 21, God's answer to the problem was to make a woman for Adam.

Why did God only make one woman? Why didn't he make two or three women and bring them to Adam to choose the one he wanted? Why was God so restrictive?

God knew that man only needed one woman—before and after marriage. God restricted him to Eve because there was only one woman that he was supposed to show his romantic side to. He didn't need two or three women to go through before he got to Eve.

If you think about it, love is a command in the Bible. And this kind of love that goes between a man and his wife is never commanded to be shown in any other relationship. In fact, it is reserved *only* for a husband and a wife. Just let that sink in for a little bit.

Nowhere should a brother and sister be in a romantic love relationship. We would all agree with that. But gentleman, let me remind you that the ladies and girls in this church are your sisters in Christ—they are not your wives. They should not be the objects of romantic interest for you.

Young ladies, you belong not involving yourself in a romantic interest with the young men of this church who are your brothers in Christ. If you do, you bring yourself and them into a defrauding relationship.

Never in the Bible are girlfriends and boyfriends even addressed, and certainly boyfriends/girlfriends loving each other in a romantic way is completely absent from scripture.

You have maybe heard the phrase from the song that says, *Breaking up is hard to do*. That is a very true statement. But it happens all the time in the dating relationship, and it happens often in the courting relationship.

Breaking up is divorce preparation. You are not preparing yourself for a committed relationship. You are learning how to say good-bye and how to walk out on a relationship this time, and next time and the next time and the next time. And no matter how many times you do it, it doesn't get any easier.

History of Dating

How in the world did we get into the dating scene? If you look at history, you will find that dating originated quite recently. It was not practiced in history all the way up until around the 1800's.

In the 18th century, there was a philosophical movement called romanticism that began to take hold and influence society. Authors lamented that western civilization had fallen into what they called the error of exalting reason over feelings. They proposed that what we needed to do was to make decisions based on emotions rather than intellect.

Before this time, love between a husband and a wife was something that was expected once they got married. But it was never expected before they got married. In fact, to marry for love was something that was not a prerequisite—it was unusual and unexpected. Men and women entered into marriage with an understanding that they were to love one another.

Today, we get married when we find someone that we love. By love, we don't mean commitment but we have redefined it to mean more of a lustful attraction, which sadly will end after you are married. When that attraction and emotion leaves, what will happen?

Love the one you marry

In Ephesians 5:25, husbands are commanded to love their wives, not their girlfriends. In Titus 2:4, the older women are to teach the younger women to love their husbands. God does not say they are to teach them to love their boyfriend. Never in the scriptures will you find this kind of love ever exchanged between a man and a woman apart from marriage, unless it is portrayed in an illicit manner and one that God condemns.

The romantics taught that you should marry the one you love. But the Christians teach that you should love the one you marry. Is there a difference? Yes, there is a major difference.

I am commanded to love my wife, and I willingly and gladly do it. But it doesn't matter if my emotions feel great—I have a command from God which keeps me committed to my marriage relationship even during difficult times which I may not always feel like it. Thankfully, when you engage your heart in the right way, and you practice God's Word, those periods of time will be fewer and further between.

But mark my words—those difficult times will come if you live together any length of time. Solomon put it this way in the Song of Solomon. Three times in that book—in 2:7, 3:5 and 8:4—the very same phrase is used. ***"I charge you, O ye daughters of Jerusalem, that ye stir not up, nor awake my love, till he please."***

What did he mean? The Shulammite maiden is talking here about not stirring up a romantic interest in Solomon. She say, "Don't go around fooling with his heart and causing him to stir up those emotions on the inside."

Dear friends, let me just warn you—you have no business messing with the heart of young people or your friends or other acquaintances by talking to them about boyfriend/girlfriend things. When you do, you are stirring their emotions up. You are stirring their heart up. You are putting them in a place of fornication and violating the word of God.

Dating is Defrauding

God talks in First Thessalonians 4:6 about defrauding your brother. We talked a little bit about this earlier. To defraud is to promise something which you have no intention of delivering.

Girls, you need to be careful and circumspect about how you interact with the opposite sex. That means the way you dress and the way you look at the boys. That means the way you wink and flirt, the coy way in which you talk to a young man, and the notes that you might write.

Guys, the same goes with you. You have no business leading a young lady on to the point to where you get their hopes up, thinking you are going to carry it further. But then you dash their hopes when you tell them, "Oh no, I didn't mean that. You misunderstood my motives."

You should have guarded yourself so you didn't stir their emotions up. You have defrauded them at that point in time. You are violating the Word of God.

In First Corinthians chapter seven, it is very clear that you are not to touch a person of the opposite sex, meaning that you ought not to stir up the emotions sexually. But defrauding goes much further than just sexual fornication. It also refers to the mere emotions of hope—maybe this will turn into a marriage—because you are leading them on.

That is what dating and courtship does. The only method I know of that bypasses that would be betrothal or arranged marriage. God says there is a clear physical line—you don't belong touching a young lady or a young man, especially one that you are in any way attracted to or they are attracted to you.

Emotional Purity

But there is also an emotional purity line. Flirting breaks that line, along with promising, deceiving, misleading someone else, enticing them along, and stirring them up. You say, "Oh, I just like being with them." The moment you sense that happening in your heart, you know immediately that you have gone over the line of emotional purity. You need to back off.

Defrauding is a matter of deceiving or misleading someone, leading someone to expect certain benefits or a certain outcome to have happen. It usually goes like this. A boy and girl start talking to one another, and pretty soon they began to like each other and enjoy each other's company. Suddenly they are an item—all the other kids will know what is going on.

The girl says, "I am not going to talk to the other boys, because he will think I am not interested in him." So she begins to stop talking to the other guys. And he stops talking to any of the other girls, because he doesn't want her to think he is interested in any other girl. They are both limiting their opportunities.

When you start limiting your opportunities, you are in a position of your heart being given away in emotional impurity. Then something happens and one or the other backs out of this budding romance and one or both wind up with broken hearts. It is evidence of defrauding. It happens time and time again.

I warn you against it. Social scientists call it *bonding*, and it does happen. According to God, the ultimate outcome of that kind of bonding is supposed to be Genesis 2:24—to become one flesh.

Yet the books of today written to instruct young people on how to date in a "Christian manner" teach you how to limit yourself physically so that you don't wind up in sexual impurity. But what they don't teach you is how to turn off the emotions, how to cut the mind off from the thoughts that come. This is especially a problem with the young men.

So our first principle is rather simple. *Have you reserved romance for a committed relationship?* That kind of romantic involvement doesn't belong in any relationship except the relationship with your husband or your wife. That is it. So dating is out, and courtship is out.

Chapter Eleven
Principle Number Two:
Is your commitment continual and not conditional?

Now we want to look at the second principle of getting to the marriage altar. *Is your commitment continual and not conditional?* Or we could ask the question this way: is your commitment one that is lasting and binding, or is it one you can back out on?

In Genesis 2:21 God took a rib from Adam. He made a woman and brought her unto Adam. And Adam was excited—we know that because he said, "Whoa, man!" He called Eve, "Bone of my bone, and flesh of my flesh." Sounds to me like he was committed to her!

It is not unusual for a young man and young lady to get involved with each other and say, "We are going to go steady." Basically that means that they are an item. No one else can date him or her—they are together.

How long? Well, until one of them decides they don't want the relationship. Or until he crosses her or she crosses him. Or until one of them says, "I am leaving because I am not getting out of this relationship what I want." In other words, you are going to try them out and then drop them like a hot potato.

Not a real flattering way to describe the dating relationship, but that is what happens most of the time. It is sad and lots of lives have been broken and hearts damaged. God says when you make a commitment to marry, it needs to be a lasting commitment and one without conditions. In Matthew 19:3-9 we find these words of Jesus.

"The Pharisees also came unto him, tempting him, and saying unto him, Is it lawful for a man to put away his wife for every cause?

And he answered and said unto them, Have ye not read, that he which made them at the beginning made them male and female,

And said, For this cause shall a man leave father and mother, and shall cleave to his wife: and they twain shall be one flesh?

Wherefore they are no more twain, but one flesh. What therefore God hath joined together, let not man put asunder.

They say unto him, Why did Moses then command to give a writing of divorcement, and to put her away?

He saith unto them, Moses because of the hardness of your hearts suffered you to put away your wives: but from the beginning it was not so.

And I say unto you, Whosoever shall put away his wife, except it be for fornication, and shall marry another, committeth adultery: and whoso marrieth her which is put away doth commit adultery."

God does not like divorce

When a man and a woman come together and become one flesh, this is more than just a physical union. It speaks of a bonding, a becoming one. A husband and wife are one in heart, one in spirit, and one in purpose.

The illustration has been used before of gluing two boards together with wood glue. Then after it has hardened and set up, you try to pull them apart. They never break just right down the seam exactly like they were before. You will have to rip them apart and the edges will be jagged. Those two boards will never fit onto another board perfectly again.

So it is with a young man or young lady's heart. They give their heart to another and then all of a sudden, their heart is ripped apart in the break-up that takes place. When they go to marry someone else, there will be jagged spots in their life, and it will affect their relationships going forward. God never intended that kind of a mess to be there in a person's life.

In verses 7 and 8 we find that the idea of divorce in the Bible was never God's invention. God was not saying, "Get rid of her because you don't like her." It was because of the hardness of people's hearts. That is the only reason divorce ever takes place.

You will find that this divorcement proceeding was only allowed during the betrothal period. During the betrothal period, if she was found to be unfaithful to her future husband, the young lady could be given a writing of divorcement. But once the marriage has been consummated, the only way that adultery could be dealt with was by stoning.

Think about it for a moment. How angry could you get at your husband or your wife to stone them? Here is how stoning took place. If you were the one making the accusation, you would pick up the first stone, and with all the people gathered around, you would throw the first stone at her to draw the first blood.

I think I would find that pretty hard to do. I mean, you might get angry at your wife, you may be very hurt over her infidelity—but to actually throw the first stone would be something very, very difficult to ever do. But that is God's pronouncement of how to end a marriage if adultery has taken place.

God desires reconciliation

Now, that is Old Testament scripture, so I am not encouraging anyone to go out and stone their spouse. But this is what I want you to see. Divorcement was left only as an option during betrothal periods. Even that was never God's preference.

God wasn't saying, "Go ahead and get rid of them." He said, "I will allow this because of the hardness of your heart. What ought to happen is forgiveness and reconciliation." That is God's answer.

What did Hosea do with his wife Gomer? She didn't just have an affair with one guy. She was a prostitute and was with many men in a visible manner in the community. It must have been very shocking and humiliating for Hosea. Yet Hosea took her back in, and God wanted him to take her back in. It would be a picture of God's kind of love for the nation of Israel.

Thus marriage also ought to be a picture of the love of Almighty God for His people. As Christians, that is how we should operate. I know the hardness of our hearts gets in the way a lot of times. But if you know Christ, you have the grace of God to help you do that.

Marriage is a commitment

This second principle speaks of commitment. This commitment is reserved for marriage. Today in our society, we have what we call engagement. During this engagement period, either the young man or the young lady has the option of breaking off the engagement if they begin to feel that they have not made a wise choice.

Broken engagements happen all the time. So it causes the young man and the young lady to not be honest with each other. They are wondering if they are going to go all the way to the marriage altar, and careful about how much they reveal to their future spouse.

In betrothal, on the other hand, a young man and a young woman decide that they are committed to marriage. When that commitment is there, then the walls can drop and they can begin to have a good relationship long before the physical union takes place after they are married. Later, when they are married, the physical part just adds a new dimension and joy to that relationship.

In dating and often in engagement what ends up happening is that the pressure for physical involvement builds. Before long, the young man and the young lady give in to that pressure and begin to be involved physically. When the physical involvement begins, all the other areas of communication shut down or at least are greatly limited. God never intended that.

Commitment bring security

This committed relationship is a relationship of security. That is God's intent. The young lady knows that the young man is going to the marriage altar with her, and they will be man and wife.

They don't have to worry about whether or not someone else is going to come in the picture, or they are going to get tired of each other, or they are going to give up on each other. They are one together, like Joseph and Mary, before they came together as husband and wife.

Commitment shows selflessness

There is a selflessness that goes with marriage, and this is where the commitment begins to show. It shows in the father who has an obligation to his daughter at the marriage. It is his job to furnish the wedding. That is the practice in Scripture at least.

The groom has an obligation to provide jewels and jewelry of silver and gold for his wife. Again that is the practice of scripture. The young man gives the woman a token of his love and commitment. That is where our practice in our culture of giving an engagement ring comes from.

Did you ever hear of a young man and young lady breaking up before they get to the marriage altar, and the guy says, "Give me back my ring?" No sir, you gave her the ring as an commitment. You have defrauded her—you owe her much more than that ring.

Another Bible practice that was carried out was the practice of a dowry. This was given by the groom to the father of the bride. This gift was his estimation of her great value and worth to him. He would give it because he valued this lady. That is the kind of selflessness that should be seen.

I have heard young men say, "I would never do that." Young man, you don't deserve to have a young lady as a wife. If her price is not far above rubies in your eyes, then you ought to not even be proposing to her. In fact, you are showing your own selfishness, and you have a real problem. You need to value the lady that God has given you.

So the second principle speaks about commitment. Are you willing to be committed to each other? The young lady is willing to say, "He is the one for me. There are no others." The young man says, "She is the one God has chosen for me. I value her highly."

Chapter Twelve
Principle Number Three
Have you entered into this relationship only with parental protection and parental permission?

The third principle for getting to the marriage altar has to do with parent's involvement. *Have you entered into this relationship only with parental protection and parental permission?*

I know the practice of the day in our culture is to disregard what the parents think. The young man and the young lady go out and find their choice, and then bring them home to introduce them to their parents. That is the cultural practice of today, but it is not a Biblical practice.

It is very clearly a sin in the Word of God to cut yourself off from parental involvement in your life. There is a parental responsibility given to them by God to guide and to guard and to give their children in marriage. It is not the job of the young people to give themselves in marriage.

I understand that we live in a generation where a lot of parents have abdicated their duties. That is the parent's fault. If you are in that situation, there are some things you can do.

The parents need to take their responsibility to guide their children. The young people also have a responsibility, and that is to allow the parents to be involved and to listen to their guidance.

The Responsibility of Parents

Recognize the Need

Genesis 2:18 teaches us that the parents have a responsibility to recognize the need. Adam had no earthly parents, so God takes that place. God saw the need for a wife for Adam. It was not Adam's idea, but God's idea. Samson, on the other hand, demanded that his parents get him a certain woman, and great trouble came from that situation.

Parents, you have a responsibility to recognize the need in your children. You should be watching them and praying for them and waiting for the time, especially for your son. And when he is ready, then you can be there to help him and to point him in a right direction.

Refining of the son

In Genesis 2:19-20 we see the refining of the son. It is the parent's job to make sure that their son is ready for married life. Parents, you need to be paying attention.

Is he ready for marriage and responsible enough to take care of a wife? Does he know how to treat her properly? Will he provide for her? Is he holding down a job and will he be diligent in that job?

I am not talking about overdoing this, but be reasonable. I know when I got married, I was not ready. God blessed our marriage in spite of that. But it is the parent's job to make sure your child is ready for marriage.

That is what God did as He placed the animals in front of Adam, watching Adam's reactions. Then God put Adam to sleep and made a woman for Adam.

Release them to their spouse

When our children get married, we need to release them to their spouse. Sometimes a young man will marry a young lady, and then the parents of either one will try to continue to control the relationship. Young people, when you get married, you are to leave father and mother. You build your own home.

Mom and Dad are nothing more than good friends and advisors if you ask. But they don't belong sticking their nose into your business. The only way you should step in is if you see your son mistreating your daughter-in-law. As a father you have the responsibility to step in and deal with him.

So remember, parents, once they are married, you have no power over their relationship. You have no business sticking your nose in where it is not wanted. They have their own family, and they don't need you telling them how to run their family. God turned Adam lose to this woman named Eve, and Adam was excited.

It is the responsibility of the father of the bride-to-be to guarantee her virginity at marriage. If fathers would adopt that a little bit in our culture today, it would change the way that fathers today interact with their daughters, and what they let their daughters do. It would change whether dads allow their daughters to be out with guys alone or not.

And if you are wondering—no, I don't believe girls ought to be out with guys alone. They don't belong there. In Bible days, there was even a price that the father had to pay if his daughter was not a virgin at marriage. He had to provide proof.

What that says to me is that fathers have serious responsibility to oversee the purity of their daughters. I think it includes not only physical purity, but emotional purity as well. God is the One who created the interest in romance. It did not take Him by surprise.

Responsibility of Young People

Give mind to parents

The young man and the young lady also have a responsibility to the parents. In Genesis 2:19-20 we notice that Adam opened up his thinking to God. He wasn't afraid to talk with God about anything and everything. Adam was brilliant and he was employing his mind—and God who was infinitely smarter than Adam let him do it.

Dads, we need to let our young people employ their minds. When you micromanage their lives, you cause great harm. But young people, you have a responsibility to give your minds to your parents. They need to hear what is going on inside. They need to understand what you are thinking—and they won't know unless you tell them. When you think out loud, they get a glimpse of what is in your heart.

Give heart to parents

Second, he gave his heart. Adam was willing to lie down and let God operate on him. He trusted God. God removed a rib from Adam. But Adam wasn't busy trying to protect himself.

Young man, you don't have any business protecting yourself from your father. You ought to welcome his involvement in your life. Your human father will make mistakes, but he has also been down the road already. And by way of observation, study of scripture, and sometimes by way of error that he has made, he has learned some lessons that can save you a lot of trouble, if you will listen.

Dads, it is not your job to micromanage and control your kids and try to force them into a relationship. But your job is to be involved in their life. Listen as they share their heart with you and give them Biblical direction.

Give hands to parents

Third, Adam opened his hand. He was willing to follow God's direction and go to sleep. When he woke up, God had a woman for him. He looked at her and was excited.

Let me make a comment here. Some have thought that betrothal is nothing more than an arranged marriage. But that is not true. In an arranged marriage, the parents have all the say, and the young people have no say. You could practice betrothal that way and force an arranged marriage upon your son or your daughter.

But for me, this is one of the most difficult places to be able to walk. As a Dad I need to be careful that I don't overstep the bounds and say to my daughter or to one of my sons, "This is who you have to marry." I have been very careful to not do that.

On the other hand, there have been times when as a father, I needed to step in and say, "No, this is not the right person for you." They may be a very good person and have good character, but they won't fit with your son or your daughter.

You have an obligation to step in and say, "No, they are not the right one for you. This is not the will of God."

Young people, you need to have a good enough relationship with your parents that you are willing to listen to their counsel. If they sense something wrong with the young man or the young lady that you are considering, you better heed their warning. Yes, you have the final say, but your parents might see something that you are missing out on.

Only betrothal fits with all three principles.

Romance is allowed only after the betrothal commithment has been made.

A betrothal commitment means they are going all the way to the marriage altar.

And parents are involved in the whole process, giving their input and guidance.

Chapter Thirteen
The Three Principles Applied

Let's go back and review all three principles and then see how the apply to the four ways in our culture of getting to the marriage altar.

Principle Number One: Have you reserved romance for a committed relationship? This principles speaks of romance, which is to be reserved only for a marriage relationship.

Principle Number Two: Is your commitment continual and not conditional? This principle speaks of commitment, which again is reserved for a marriage relationship and is to be binding.

Principle Number Three: Have you entered into this relationship only with parental protection and parental permission? The third principle has to do with parental involvement in the process—to protect and to guide and to give their approval.

Dating Fails

So let's go back and consider each principle and see how dating stack up? Well, if the first principle is followed, and we evaluate dating, we know that dating fails on that count. Dating is all about romance.

If we look at the second principle, we have to say that dating fails again. There is no commitment with dating.

And the third principle fails with dating. If you have a parental supervised dating, I suppose you could say that the young lady is somewhat protected. But you have failed on the other two principles.

So dating fails on all three principles. Dating is not something that

Christian young people should be involved in. If your children are involved in dating, I urge you to consider the principles that we have talked about here. Don't let them destroy their lives and their future marriages.

Courtship Fails

How about courtship? How does it measure up? It also fails on the first principle, because there is romance involved with courtship.

The two young people are hoping that it will end in marriage, but knowing that the relationship could be broken. It is not a committed relationship. So it fails on the second principle also.

You could say under courtship that certainly the parents are involved, but still the other two principles have been violated.

Arranged Marriage Fails

If you look at arranged marriage, you violate the third principle. Protection and permission is just that—it is not an order, which is what you have in arranged marriage. The two young people have no say in the matter.

Betrothal Fits all Three Principles

Only betrothal fits with all three principles. Romance is not allowed until the betrothal commitment has been made. A betrothal commitment means they are going all the way to the marriage altar. And parents are involved in the whole process, giving their input and guidance.

How to Practice Betrothal

Many people have asked, "How should we practice betrothal?" Let me just say that I don't have all the answers. Many people don't like the word "betrothal" and they may follow the principles but call it something else. That is no problem. The important thing is that the principles of God's Word are followed.

In a betrothal relationship, this is how it ideally should happen. The young man and his dad should be in communication with each other. The dad has determined that the young man is ready for marriage. He has shown himself consistent and faithful and charactered, and he has a job and can take of a wife. He is going to treat her right.

So, the father approaches his son and tells him, "Son, it is time for us to start praying for a young lady for you." It may take 6 months, or it may take 6 years. But you begin to pray together.

When the right young lady comes along, it may be the young man who notices her or it may be the father. Or it could be the mother of the young man. It doesn't really matter. They begin by observing her character. What kind of character does she have?

Don't jump into this too quickly by just going to talk to her. No, that can cause much hurt. Check out the character. You look at character first, then you look at personality.

Some young man might say, "What if I get stuck with some ugly girl that I don't even like?" Well, that is why you have veto power. Just say, "No, Dad, I am not interested." I am not suggesting that a guy has to marry somebody that they are not attracted to.

There are ways to find out what her true character is, especially when you are dealing with a young lady that you have not been around very much. One way is by working through the character qualities worksheet. (Available for download here: ***http://www. purposedcoachingblog.com/CharacterQualitiesCheckList.pdf.***) The goal is to know the character of that young lady.

At that point, if the parents of the young man are satisfied that this young lady is right, and the young man is satisfied that she is the right young lady, then and only then is an approach to be made to the parents of the girl. The approach is not made to the young lady, but to her parents.

The parents of the young lady, because they have veto power, can then pray about it. Parents, be sensitive to the feelings of the young man. Don't just say "No" right away, but give it a serious season of prayer.

If you don't feel that it is the will of God after you have prayed about it, then go back to them and tell them, "We don't believe that this is the will of God." What I have found that often happens at this point is the young man asks, "Why?"

Father, you don't have to give him a reason why. Just say, "We have prayed about it. She is my daughter, I am her father, and I said no. That is all you need to know. End of story."

The young man may push and really wish to know—I think that is only natural. But young man, let me say that you probably don't really want to know their reason. Besides, you need to be concerned about pleasing God and He may have just spared you from a marriage that would have been a big heartache for you.

If God wanted it worked out, He would have worked it out. And if she is the right young lady for you and the Lord wants to work it out later, then you just need to be patient.

If the parents decide that this might be the right young man for their daughter, the next step depends on how well they know the young man. If they know the character of the young man well enough and can recommend him to their daughter, then they approach their daughter.

What if you don't know the young man well enough? This is where the dad gets involved. I don't recommend a 30 minute session where you just sit down and ask him a few questions. If it is a young man that I do not know, I am going to want to spend more time with him that that. I need to know what his character is like.

I am going to find out about his life. I am going to observe him and watch him and put him in situations where he is going to be tested. I need to know how he treats people and how he handles problems.

How does he treat his mother and his sisters? How does he treat the waitress? How does he handle problems in his life? As a father, I am going to be concerned about those things.

When I am ready to say that this young man is marriageable, then I can go to my daughter and ask her to pray about it. She has three choices. She can say no, and the whole thing ends there. She has every right to say no—it is her life. She is the one that is has to marry the guy.

Second, she might say, "I don't know him well enough yet." If that is the case, there is a way for her to discover his character—not his romantic ability but his character. She needs to know more about the young man's character to know whether he is the right person for her.

Again, let me recommend the character qualities worksheet to help in this analysis. It is available for download here: *http://www. purposedcoachingblog.com/CharacterQualitiesCheckList.pdf.*

If however she knows it is God's will, and this is the man that God wants her to marry, that is good. She can say yes and the betrothal can go forward.

For an further in-depth teaching on betrothal and how to carry it out, see my book, *The Seven Steps to the Marriage Altar: How to Practice the Principles of Betrothal,* available for purchase here: *http://www.purposedcoachingblog.com/about/ebooks-by-doug-hammett/seven-steps-to-the-marriage-altar-how-to-practice-the-principles-of-betrothal/*

Conclusion

Parents, you might think that this all seems so hard. Well, let me just tell you that it is a lot of work. Emotions are not easy things. Ruling your emotions is hard work. But you can't just throw your emotions away—that will only cause heartache. When you finally get married, you are going to be uncontrollable.

Young man, if you can't control your own emotions, you don't belong even considering marriage. That is a pre-requisite. The terminology in the Bible is like this—you need to go to sleep. You need to be able to put your own heart to sleep, until God wakes you up and says, "It is time."

Young people, you need to yield your heart to Christ and use your single years to serve God. God does not tell us these things because He wants to hurt us or harm us or make us miserable in life. He tells us these things because His way is best. I want God's way for my kids, and for my grandkids. And I want God's way for you and your kids and grandkids too—because it is best.

Parents, it starts with you and I. Protecting our kids, teaching our kids, and preparing our kids so that they can be ready to walk through this process the best way possible—and in a way that is pleasing God. Let's dare to do that.

www.ingramcontent.com/pod-product-compliance
Lightning Source LLC
Chambersburg PA
CBHW071832020426
42331CB00007B/1694